Harvesting The Weather

Harvesting The Weather

Jo Heather

First published 2017
by Mudfog Press
c/o Beacon Guest Farm
Chop Gate,
Stokesley.
TS9 7JS
www.mudfog.co.uk

Copyright © Jo Heather (Jo Briggs)
All rights reserved

Cover Design by Alan Turnbull.

Print by Evoprint & Design Ltd.

ISBN: 978-1-899503-97-1

*For our children and grandchildren
and those who come after.*

*And I have watched faces returning
Down a flight of rooms for want of light.*
David Constantine 'Hyacinth'

Contents

9 At Home With Heirlooms
10 Flood
11 Indian Summer
12 Superstar: Averil At Teatime
13 Even So
14 Summer Colour
16 Beauty Flies
17 Antique Chest
18 If Only I Had One
19 Lemon
20 My Mother's Hands
21 Coming Home
22 Stoat
23 My Mother's Wardrobe
24 Reparation
25 My Father's Brother 1939
26 Grandma's Other Son
27 Dining Room 1950
28 Swimming At The Boys' School
29 Imagine
30 1962
31 Dancing
32 Delphi
33 Singer Sewing Machine
34 As If I Needed To Remind Her
36 Out Of My Depth
38 To A Bracelet
39 After Harvest
40 Firstborn
41 Birthday, Winter Morning
42 Accident
43 Boy On A Bike
44 Transplanted

45 Planting Dandelions
46 Rose Diplomacy
47 With Astrid And The Children At Yarm Fair
48 Domestic
49 Jack
50 Writing About The Lost Concert
51 About Snow
52 Back End

At Home With Heirlooms

The magical rugs my grandmother left,
with the worn cloth tags saying Qatar on the back
I treated badly, or the children did,
scuffing and fighting over 30 years. I rolled them -

unencumbered I could start again -

into the attic. Now, in this sudden, soaring May
the mould spores there are up to no good,
turning rose and coral and turquoise to black.
I unfurl them from the dark like butterflies -

a desert without colour now my days -

and spread them on gravel, dry as Arabia,
let the strict sun kill off the rot. Redolent
of flowery meads, they'll glow in the shade
of rose-petalled rooms, to last my life out -

so rich the design hidden in dust.

Once, I made sense of those squared-off birds,
chevron and lozenge and triangle-tree.
Perhaps they are symbols of paradise: clues
to a better, and kinder, and quieter life.

I need to relearn a language I've lost.

Flood

On Bilsdale Moor and on Arden
again the heather spreads
in lakes of amethyst.

Down the hills new gullies stream
like wounds
dried brown by the August sun.

A summer ago that moorland
exploded
like a dam breached.

In the creeks, great trees
were hurled into pyres.

Hawnby church a rock
in a black tide.

Grass lost in a shroud of silt,
and tombstones flung like toys.

Unharvested the June hay hangs
on hedge and taut wire.

But grass in churchyard and pasture
springs back,
wall-high already.

Indian Summer

June left behind, our midsummer monsoon,
blackberries the sweetest they've ever been,
September sun low but never so bright.
Geoff has shined my windows to match.

The Joneses are not splitting up, he says.
He does the windows. He knows a lot.
The insurance is through: Fred will be back
in his house before winter, this week Far End
gets the roof on, and Sue at the forge
has floor tiles blue as this sapphire sky.

Rowans are studded with rubies; briars
advance like barbarians over the wall;
fruit stains veranda steps with blood.
High-handed summer rides out like a rajah.

Superstar: Averil At Teatime

My mother sits bowed, part of the chair, a heap
of soft cushions, a drift of misplaced
autumn leaves, her knees and shoulders draped
in brown rug and pashmina. I observe
her faded hazel eyes, her parchment skin.

And yet any moment she will fling aside her years,
run to the kitchen saying it's time for tea, and the tray
will be here, her feathery scones, her sharp summer jam.

But today, guess what, she's different. New clothes:
creamy shirt, skirt with big flowers,
Maxmara jacket in raspberry red:
she blossoms in her chair like a rose.

Superstar is the name of a favourite rose

Even So

No summer of free flight,
I know, transformed
to rainbow-light from chrysalis-dark:
I carry my whole life with me.

My house is earthy but fits me well
and is comforting to hide in.

Why lose the past?
It isn't too heavy and I climb easily
slow, slow up

the reaching stalks
of iris and larkspur. Their blue and white
is enough of sky for me.

Summer Colour

1

I'm trying different hair,
to go with my mother-of-the-groom dress
which is an undecided colour that suited me
when was young.

Lynne is confident, takes
each faded strand in turn and brushes
pink chalky paint
over the squares of tin. Her fingers
never falter; the foil
never skids to the floor,
is folded and clipped in place.
I'm spiky, metal-helmeted,
time-travelling back to a new, old, me:
my hair will be its true colour again,
red-glinting in the sun.

Then I remember Alice
and gardeners painting white roses red.
In Wonderland.

II

I'm tying back the Rosa Gallica -
is it New Dawn?
I think the colour
too strong a pink for that -
which has slipped its moorings,
my feeble lashings of garden twine.

I tug and curse. Elastic sprays
weighted with June jump back
out of my grasp, draw blood.

But I'm determined to see
the full dark blooms up in the wind,
their power known far off,
and see, below, the water pulse
from the old grey millstone, and a rose armada
harboured there.

Beauty Flies

In the warm garden
Harvest asters,
a purple feast for bees
and a storm
of unexpected butterflies

from forty years ago
caught on my mothers buddleia
and stilled
in the ammonia jar to keep
as long as childhood:

peacock, red admiral,
small tortoiseshell
and I recognise
now I'm older
a painted lady too.

Beautyflies, they fly
fragments of that rainbow
so soon faded
from the Wainstones.
Heaven in ordinarie

Antique Chest

Dark-stained, long and low, maybe
old and Jacobean, maybe pretending,
the top reinforced with struts and edged
with curlicues. On top an oval mirror propped.

In the gilded frame I see myself daily
put on a braver face. My lipsticks jostle
with brushes, hairspray, scent; my horde
of necklaces and rings sprawls dustily.
.
Inside are clothes I wore when you were ill,
laid out in careful folds. They're too young
for me now. And my favourites of yours;
how could I forget which ones?

Maybe the soft linen shirt I gave you,
maybe the rumpled chinos, the dark jacket
that got too big for you. If I raise the lid
who will come out dressed in our clothes?

If Only I Had One

I want a coat like Henry the VIII
all sleeve, worth a fat king's ransom,
with sapphires like a summer of heat
and mellow with moonlight pearls.

It will of course be blooded with rubies
but diamonds will spark there like shooting stars
and the cuffs will be soft with hedgerow flowers,
white lilac, primroses, Queen Anne's Lace.

I will flaunt my coat when I need a suitable
sleeve to wear my heart on.

Lemon

I have spoilt this perfect fruit, sunny and firm,
sliced pale crescents for my gin and tonic.

The moon last night was a slice of lemon,
bright and sharp and cool - Artemis,

paradoxical goddess of nurture and cruelty,
governing our conception and our blood

who drives the sea and our reason so they say.
Wolf-baying, mind-altering queen of the night!

Everyone's mother. Mine matched her
in distance, in power; her opinions were

barbed as lemon juice, her lemon meringue
an irresistible peace offering.

My mother - contrary as this lemon which holds
moon and sun in its glowing skin.

My Mother's Hands

At twenty six they're already knobbly,
the knuckles a fan of spanner heads
arming her for women's work.
Her hair is rolled tight, 40s' style,
sandals blancoed chalky-white.

They sit close, she and my father,
on a light-filled verandah at Isipingo Beach;
I see jacarandas, the maid's bright headscarf.
On her knee my mother holds me balanced,
her loving focus, though my father narrows
English eyes not used to so much sun.

Soon they will board a troop ship, sail away
to his grey country, to pale bottled gooseberries,
dried egg, margarine, porridge, Virol,
where anthracite runs out before winter,
to rooms with doors tight shut against draughts.

She will feel her veins freeze even in June,
see her fingers whiten with Raynaud's. But
for sixty more years, strong as tempered steel,
her hands will serve; help her live,
teach, keep her careful accounts
and make an English garden full of colour.

Coming Home

As early as she dares my mother walks to town -
past the newsagent (open), the butcher (shut)

across the rush hour traffic-river and up
Barnfield Hill under white blossom trees.

She skirts the crumbling Roman walls,
stooped on swollen feet, walks steadily on,

fills her trolley - not too full to steer:
Kerrygold from Sainsbury's (only the best)

coffee cake from Marks (she no longer bakes),
a mango from the market, an avocado pear.

She thinks of the place where they grew on trees
and you had papaya for breakfast every day.

She gets the bus (someone always heaves her shopping on)
and, indoors again, sets the fruit on the window sill:

sunshine colours from her girlhood
grainy gold and peach, smooth alligator green.

Stoat

Yesterday my mother,
hearing the news,
attacked my son for saying they didn't need
to be married, and savaged
his girlfriend leaving her for dead.
As if the unseen baby,
illegitimate,
could jeopardise our survival.

I've seen her slipping between stone and groundsel,
self-effacing in her caramel coat.
I imagine her pouncing
leopard-like on a vole
who happens to cross her path,
needle-teeth fastening. Blood.

My Mother's Wardrobe

had belonged to her mother:
no taller than me, dark wood, an architrave
carved with peacocks, lilies embossed
on the looped, brass handle-mounts.
The long glass in the door was dimmed
by age and reflected only shadows.
You weren't supposed to look inside.

I found work blouses, dowdy skirts; the scent
of her *Je Reviens*; nothing
surprising. Then, at the very back,
a trailing satin nightdress,
cloud-blue, soft as a ghost;
and the secret skin of the wardrobe:
ruched silk, dark red, voluptuous.

Reparation

A useful small bookcase my father made
from hardwood and ply, tall and sturdy,
its curved top lovingly finished.
It stood in the playroom corner,
in the place between
all the children's growing and his decline.

No Hepplewhite, is it!
I once too carelessly remarked. I caused him
damage I could never repair.
In this house now it will always hold
his Shakespeare, his Chambers, Dickens and Scott
and fill a place in our very best room.

My Father's Brother 1939

I've often thought: was it an obsession
with trains, a clockwork engine buzzing
round the track with nowhere to go?
Or an obsession with journeys, obscure
Dorset hamlet to the channel beaches,
infinite water and questioning gulls,
the carriage doors thudding like a deadmarch,
and triumphant letting go of steam?

An obsession perhaps with the Heroic:
Boys' Own Paper brave Boy Scouts and upright
Schoolboys (*mens sana in corpore sano*)
defeating the Hun? And was his life
pointless (murmuring heart unfit to serve)?
What drove him through the whirling night to catch
the friendly train whose whistle summoned him
to jump before it shuddered to a halt?

Grandma's Other Son

On my grandparents' sideboard a young man
taken in profile - black hair, aquiline nose,
an avoiding eye - someone strange, not breathing.

The photos at home are alive: Mummy and Daddy
in their bedroom, very smiley in separate frames
her in pearls, him in uniform after that war.

Downstairs in the sunny living room Ginny and me
together in our party dresses Mummy made
with frills and big sashes. She is all curls and mischief,

I am shy with sober scraped back hair. We
are stopped there before time works the lines
on cheek and eyelid that write a life.

Time that will rub us out and leave
only a frame, grey paper, an evasive ghost.

Dining Room 1950

Earth-smell from the scullery: hen food, coalgas.
Black Rayburn, its red mica window locked.
Alcoved books, my erudite father's: best
are the blue with gold crests saying form prize.
Table, with wolves' feet, of makora wood -
it came in a big crate the water got in;
a cut-glass jug full of daffs hides the stain.
Matched sideboard, framed jacarandas above.

Margarine, marmite - Cape gooseberry jam
Aunt Margaret brought the day she came back
from shining Johannesburg; tall as a crane
she writes for her life like virginia Woolf.
She talks to my father. I listen. Out
in the kitchen my mother flutters and fumes.

Swimming At The Boys' School

Water was our element. All summer term
we practised every evening before tea
in the long outdoor pool. We didn't feel
the cold, as we thrashed length after length,
two slim seals in our regulation black.
We took no notice of fifth-form boarders
ogling from windows on the school's top floor.

White-helmeted, buoyant and fearless, we
kept our heads down not thinking of ruined hair,
and breathed in time with our beating arms and feet.
And hearts. Untouched for one last summer

Imagine

an idyllic scene,
A warm pool in a warm country.
Four little girls at home in the water.
Bougainvillea matches my swimsuit.
Palm trees shade the side
where mums and dads are watching us.
We liked it there,
Janet, Angela, Mary and I,
much nicer than our baths at home
all steam and chlorine
making our eyes red.

Mary's dad died when she was 10.
How could she go on playing and not cry?
Then Janet's brother, the eldest,
drowned in the river.
She said they never got over it:
we tried to understand.
Angela's father died young,
but we were older then,
had exams to aim for, boyfriends.

For this moment we float
on deep blue water,
making a star.

1962

The last summer at school, we're standing,
Head Girl Janet and all my friends
arms round each other, laughing. Prefects
in our boaters and black stockings,
acting responsible we broke the rules
like anyone else when no-one would find out.

I scraped through A-Level, my mind fixed
on boys. At the Young Conservatives I met
students who seemed like men, fell for Terry
working class and cockney-accented - shock horror -

settled for Peter who wasn't. He was 25 and drank,
but Mummy and Daddy didn't know that.

But best was blonde Rick, somebody's brother
home from the merchant navy. He
took me jiving, and for my first meal out - Chinese,
and to 'the pictures', 2 bob in the double seats
back row of the old Theatre Royal, his arm
creeping round my shoulders.

He tried it on, well they all did that.
Years before the Pill, going all the way
was strictly for marriage - one rule
it was too dangerous to break.

Dancing

Think of me with - what was his name?
Magical dancer, fairy prince.
I was possessed
with the demon joy of the dancing.

Later - days? Weeks? We were in the back seat
of his mother's car on Haldon Common
with night-black fir trees closing in,
and I wouldn't.

I suppose I never saw him again.
I remember his hair
like dark silk, and a spell
broken

Delphi

That summer I abandoned my engagement
and went south to Ancient Greece,
to the Parthenon and the Peloponnese,
and with any luck romance.
I smothered my face with make-up
(no factor50 in those days)
to protect my nose from sunburn
 - not a good look.

We toured in an oven on wheels
to Olympia: sad white fallen statues
and a cafe stapled to the mountainside
over a valley so deep it looked bottomless.
To Delphi: grass, olive trees broken pillars.
And where was the oracle?

I could have asked, Who will marry me now?

Singer Sewing Machine

It made fun clothes for the Swinging Sixties:
simple scoop necks, no top stitching,
not much skirt; once, a needlecord pinafore
in sophisticated black worn
daringly with no blouse.

But for 30 years tied to the treadmill
of motherhood I abandoned it:
clothes were cheaper and smarter snatched
from the rails at C&A.
I never taught my daughter to sew.

But now I have found sweet rag dolls
with black button eyes and round red cheeks,
one each for Rosie 4 and Esme 3;
and patterns for dolls' dresses
simple to make, glamorous to wear.

So I escape to my cotton reels, scissors and pins.
The machine whirrs, a dress appears,
jazzy with rickrack and daisy chains,
so Esme and Rosie can play at being mothers,
never dreaming of one day being me

As If I Needed To Remind Her
To my sister

As if yesterday I see her
in her denim jacket
smoking, tapping ash
over the parapet,
the full moon above,
the small black river snaky below.
Which will she choose, moon or river?
She will make it one way or another.

I

My attic at home, its big window looking west
to Haldon across the Exe and the railway line,
became yours - the horsehair sofa, the Rubaiyat.
They forgot it ever had been mine.

Later you really needed it.
Too soon you were in hospital nearing the end
and I slept there again surrounded by your things.
There comes a time when dying
mustn't be put off: you kept on saying 'I'm so pathetic.'
You died at midnight, our mother's birthday.

Alone in the house with my tiny children
I woke in the dead hours, searing pain around my heart.
I smothered panic, propped pillows to breathe, waited
for dawn. The phone call came then.

II

I was the oldest supposed to be grown-up and good.
I tried to run away at hairwash time.
Lux flakes mixed in a jug, soap in my eyes
stinging and stinging even if I held the flannel tight.
Mummy always in a hurry, not gentle.

You were the good one.
Little sister, I never really knew you

III

You swung into the sixties,
the soberer seventies. Bridge over Troubled Water
played at your wedding, you in a white satin trouser suit
you made yourself, he in green velvet.
But he wasn't good to you.

You started to get headaches, and fall over in the street:
thing growing in your skull.
Surgery. Radiotherapy. Remission.
The cancer taking hold.

He ran away.

Mother took you in.
For your last months she kept you
from the phone, made you a child again
safe in our attic.

Little sister, only sister
I never found the words to say.

Out Of My Depth

I

She was an outpatient now: I went to her home.
Her grey husband worried about her,
left us to talk alone.
She trusted me,
brought coffee, sharp rye bread
and marmite softened with butter.

Dr Little had told me her despair vanished
the day he goaded her till she screamed.
But she certainly wouldn't tell him this, she said:
One night in the park a man
pinned her against the railings,
his hand over her mouth. Forced her.
The worst thing
 - her puzzled brown eyes held mine -
Was that I enjoyed it.
Am I very wicked?

I don't remember what I said.
Did I fail her?
I was only twenty;
I know I told nobody,
and that she told the truth.

II

Dr Little is young and fat and not wise. He likes
boys with blonde curls who take heroin.
He doesn't like Jhaved.
Jhaved misses his mother back home; his father's
too hard on him, doesn't understand.
Jhaved thinks I do. He gives me
a gold propelling pencil and takes
rat poison the next day.

To A Bracelet

You went to dances, cocktails,
Polo, Bridge, even tiger shoots,
a sliver of moon on grandmother's wrist.
After she died I treasured you.

Your old country was apricots,
mangoes and pungent heat, your backdrop
the improbable Himalayas
and the steelworks at Burnpore.

Transplanted to Yorkshire chill
pictures worked on your silver face
reminded me: tiny elephants, women
demure in saris, a spike-leaved tree.

You'd worn well over the years.
When fetching logs or planting bulbs
or doing the washing up
I felt your reliable grip.

So why did I take you off
and let you slip
into the dark?

After Harvest
For Sarah and Paula

October, just, and the weather chancy.
Alone I climb Nab Ridge as serious rain begins.

The bracken's grown into a forest,
dense though the fronds are rusting,

and behind me on the slope of Hawnby Moor
the heather's long gone over.

I beat the bracken down with my stick;
slither where black stems tangle.

I'm soaked to the bone and cold.

Not like the time when I saw you both,
daughters or nymphs or angels, clear

from half a mile away against hot purple
in your summer white and cream, and ran

up the tinder path, my sandals winged,
to greet you bringing home the bilberries.

Such tiny dull blue globes,
such astonishing crimson juice.

Firstborn

In the half-dark of the nightlight,
his small warm cheek against my skin,
silence cocoons us, as he is cocooned
in his grandmother's flannelette shawl,
hand crochet-edged pale gold; his head
is pale gold and the fontanelle
pulses with his sucking, his heartbeat
rhythmic and strong.

Why should there be crying? Except
in a faraway cot with bright lights
machines and tubes, his twin survives;
tiny, monkey-faced, fluttering-hearted,
he is lifted by other safe arms, a nurse
who gently angles the feed and knows
his tongue will flop and block the way
if she doesn't help him.

Birthday, Winter Morning

Only a year from forty now you two
and in your prime, grappling with mountains,
sure-footed, steering a rock-filled course, while
I decline toward my three score years and ten.

The sun's not up, and constellations form
a pattern different from midnight stars.
How many thousand times this planet's turned
since you first saw the world my Gemini

at Candlemas! How many till the one
I shall not see? So, year by year I'll keep
a count; and light the candles to set high
in my dark house where morning's slow to shine.

And then you'll come, wheeling from your far sphere,
sunlit, starlit, not afraid of the dark.

Accident

Trying to catch a stickleback
from the high stone wall
where the water falls
the small boy wobbles
on a tipping flagstone.

A mile away on the valley road
the loud motor bikes chase
towards Fangdale
and another inevitable crash.
The rescue helicopter
rumbles overhead.

Somehow I know
the serious, balancing boy
won't fall,
that one day he'll net a stickleback and see
a dragonfly startle over the water.

Boy On A Bike

The mean road undulates and swerves
avoiding again the longed-for sea, although
gulls swoop to prove it's there.

He thinks there'll always be one more hill
between him and where he's going to

Transplanted

Bluebells? Move as many as you like.
My beasts can't eat them either, he says.
He flails at invading bracken fronds,
as if not knowing it takes more than that.
He's owned this hill, its blue and green and bronze,
for more than half a century.

I fetch my trowel and red plastic bowl, dig
where the ground's bruised by cattle,
and lift white bulbs like pearls.
Their leaves droop, discouraged.
Bedded in, sheltered by my young trees,
some of them will like it here

Not all the new hens are happy:
the restless, flighty ones,
the black and white,
have decamped onto the moor
to roost in the great hawthorn.
He says frost and snow will drive them home.

I read your letters again,
try to understand
where you are now.
The goldfish and the silver carp
undulate and dart around their pond,
busy, serene, unquestioning.

Planting Dandelions

Clive is planting dandelions in the top field -
don't laugh -
because John Rees the expert
says they are *top nosh* for bees.

Known as 'the perfect weed', and called
Devil Root by some, who'd have thought
their plain faces held such power?
Though anyone could see a distant field rivals
the spread gold of daffodils, cowslips, buttercups.

Look close and marvel: starburst petals
tapered like tiny spatulas, ringed
in perfect symmetry, a rough and thready
middle and, yes, the honey scent of Spring.

Later, their silver parachutes will drop
largesse, to seed unending
nectar for bees, ambrosia for us.

Rose Diplomacy

They're out of control and dangerous, my roses
muscle-bound and unresponsive to concessions.
I can't wait till Lady Day to tackle them; nor hope
to sow my bitter herbs by an auspicious moon.

Others before me tried to improve things,
introduce roses with a different outlook.
But Masquerade and Superstar had spread
a sort of tiredness in the soil, blighting their lives.

So it's Total War. And a question
 - with thick snake roots wired deep -
of picks and axes, allies, reinforcements. Dynamite.

There's got to be a better way.
Insinuate plants of the right calibre: tough
buddleia Black Knight or Royal Red; resourceful
sword lily; lupins, poppies, peonies, home-loving
and with a way of getting on with one another.

With Astrid And The Children At Yarm Fair

We'd been sucked in by a whirlwind -
orange, lime green, purple;
by thumping music;
sucked into into a battle scrum, with Valkyries
riding us down.
You all urged me on, wild-eyed, laughing:
It's wicked, it's to die for!

In Astrid's quiet kitchen now
she makes peppermint tea and we talk.
You are busy with your grown-up lives.
Do you remember Yarm Fair? She asks
I remember her warm kitchen afterwards,
sausages, toffee and gingerbread.

People we've loved
died yesterday
and will die tomorrow.

The hurdy gurdy music plays,
the horses' painted nostrils flare.

Domestic
after Michael Hamburger

I look out from the kitchen window
between Nigella and Delia,
mug-trees, the salt crock, various bottles.
I'm unenthusiastic about lunch.

There are the two black Marans on the lawn.
I'm pleased to see them, burnished and stately,
confronting February, feathers unruffled
though glancing white as the wind catches.

Last week the rust-winged Rhode Island too.
Gentle soul, food now for crows.
I'm thankful for my Amazonian Marans
harvesting the weather.

Jack

Each Tuesday, there he was -
bright eyed as a small brown bird,
a thrush singing his heart out -
cornerstone of the choir.
Over the months his back bent low,
formed a crotchet rest.

But then - a birthday crescendo and Jack
joining us on the concert platform;
the 90 candles on the cake,
the scores of congratulations.

March into April.
Diminuendo

We share the saddest news;
The heart has gone out of the choir.

Not far from here a ruined abbey raises
its spare frame, once shaped
for the spirit, for chant, for service.
Its great stones sustain
the walls of houses we live in.

And in our rainy gardens
a thrush, unseen, is singing.

Writing About The Lost Concert

This white paper blank as a field of snow.
November snow falling for days. The year dying
young.
In the gardens, in the trees, no singing birds, no wind.

For us, no singing tonight,
no sighing strings no high flutes or oboes
crying requiem, no Sanctus soaring.
Poor recompense, these words
black on the white paper.

We struggled today. An orchestra, a choir, dared
the iced byroads, the slowed up motorways.
Had struggled for months daring
strange cadences reaching out to a holy city.

Now, we must leave the church
before night falls with the deadness of snow.
We drive away, a mute cortege.
In our hearts the music settles.

Our scores are handed in,
black symbols on a white page under a pall of snow
By the field edge I see
a yellow maple gleam suddenly gold.

About Snow

You suddenly can't get out in the car
to go to choir or buy potatoes.
And what if you were deep in love?
You'd have an epic walk to find each other.

It doesn't suit my poor hens
any more than me.
One is trekking the cold desert of lawn
Like a hero bold
sinking stiff claws in;
she leaves a telltale line
of wonky stars.

But I love what is warm in it:
the hyacinth light
north above the Wainstones in the afternoon,
the daffodil light
against the High Moor south,

and everywhere all day
the scintillating white
fierce as angels wings.

Back End

September in one week of rain turned
summer's edge to rust: autumn too soon
taking over, reminding us of endings.

October dressed asters in purple,
prickled grass with sweet chestnuts, set fire
to rowan and oak and struck maples to gold.

November is now and we know it. Leaves lie
sopping and smell of rivers; cows wear mud.
Poor things. We must make our own fires.

Notes

The epigraph is from David Constantine's poem
'Hyacinth' in A Brightness to Cast Shadows 1980

Butterflies - After Pauline Stainer.

Averil at Teatime - Superstar is a deep salmon-pink
hybrid tea rose.

Lemon - Inspired by Catriona O'Reilly's poem
'Pollen'in The Sea Cabinet 2006.

Flood and Indian Summer refer to the 2005 flood
which swept away Hawnby Bridge and inundated
villages as far away as Sutton under Whitestonecliff

Domestic - suggested by Michael Hamburger's
'Jackdaws' in Flashlight, Northern House pamphlets
1965

Marans - a breed of hen named after the town of
France where they were bred.

Acknowledgements

A big Thank You to my family and friends (too many to name) for their encouragement and to my fellow poets for their patient support and sensitive criticism, in particular Geoff Strange and the Hall Garth Poets; the Madingley Masterclass; David Smith and the Stokesley U3A Creative Writing Class.

Thanks too to tutors of workshops where some of these poems started out, notably Mandy Sutter and Roger Garfitt - and (in no particular order) Ellen Phethean, Tara Bergin, Peter Sansom, Colette Bryce and Tamar Yoseloff.

Extra special thanks to Jackie Litherland and Pauline Plummer for their invaluable help in preparing the poems for publication. And to you Marilyn.

Photograph by Pat Maycroft

Jo Heather (Jo Briggs)

Was born in South Africa with Irish, Scottish and West Country antecedents . She grew up in Devon and, now retired from mental health social work, lives with her husband on the edge of the North York Moors. Jo has been involved with the editing, publishing and performing of poetry in the Tees Valley and North Yorkshire for many years.

Previous Publications
'Gold', pamphlet, Mudfog Press 2001 revised and reprinted 2007, and a collection 'Knowing the Dark', Indigo Dreams Press 2011
Poems in Anthologies:
'Smelter' Mudfog Press 2003 (eds. Cynthia Fuller and Kevin Cadwallender) and 'Ink on Paper' Mima/ Mudfog 2008 ed Colette Bryce